FOOLPROOF MEDITERRANEAN COOKERY

CLAUDIA RODEN

CLAUDIA RODEN

Step by step to
everyone's favourite
Mediterranean recipes

Dedication

For my children, Simon, Nadia and Anna, and their families.

Food photography by Jean Cazals

Published by BBC Worldwide Ltd,
Woodlands, 80 Wood Lane,
London W12 0TT

First published 2003

Copyright © Claudia Roden 2003
The moral right of Claudia Roden to be identified as the author of this work
has been asserted.

Food photography © Jean Cazals 2003

ISBN 0 563 53496 6

All rights reserved. No part of this book may be reproduced in any form or
by any means without permission in writing from the publisher, except by
a reviewer who may quote brief passages in a review.

Commissioning editors: Nicky Copeland and Rachel Copus
Project editor: Sarah Lavelle
Copy editor: Jane Middleton
Art direction and design: Lisa Pettibone
Home economist: Marie Ange Lapierre
Stylist: Sue Rowlands

The publishers would like to thank the following for supplying items used in the
photographs: David Mellor, Divertimenti, Kara Kara and Sumerill and Bishop.

Set in Univers
Printed and bound in Italy by L.E.G.O. spa
Colour separations by Kestrel Digital Colour, Chelmsford

Contents

Ingredients and Equip

INGREDIENTS

All ingredients used in Mediterranean cooking are generally available in the UK. Below is some useful information on the ingredients featured in this book.

Aubergines

The aubergine is the favourite vegetable of the Mediterranean. Choose firm, medium-sized ones with shiny, unblemished skin. If you are not going to fry them, you do not need to salt them to remove their bitter juices. The aubergines produced these days are only pleasantly bitter. Salting them does, however, mean that they absorb a little less oil, which is an advantage as they normally soak up so much. Grilling and roasting aubergines is a good way of avoiding that.

Bread

In the Mediterranean bread is present at every meal. It is used to pick up morsels of food, to dip into a creamy salad and to soak up sauces. It goes at the bottom of a juicy salad and in a bowl of soup; it is pounded into a sauce with olive oil; and crumbs are sprinkled over a gratin. The simplest appetizer in the western Mediterranean is a slice of bread smeared with olive oil and rubbed with garlic or tomatoes, or spread with an olive and anchovy paste.

The variety of breads that you find in the area, from the very thin, floppy breads baked on a griddle in the eastern Mediterranean to the great, round loaves of southern Italy, is extraordinary. The ever-increasing range available here is already substantial. Apart from the flat, pouched pitta, Italian ciabatta and focaccia, Spanish *pan gallego* and French baguette and country breads you can find in supermarkets, ethnic shops (mainly Turkish, Lebanese and Cypriot) and specialist bakeries now sell a wide variety of Mediterranean breads. There are different kinds of Lebanese flat breads, some exquisitely thin and light, some sprinkled with wild thyme, sesame seeds and sumac or flavoured with onions or garlic and herbs; Turkish sesame rings and huge, thick, soft, flat breads like focaccia; Greek olive breads and sesame loaves; Spanish *pan de borona* made with maize flour; Italian herb and olive oil and walnut and raisin breads.

Bulgur

Bulgur, a staple of Turkey and the Arab world, is wheat that has been boiled and dried, then ground to various degrees of fineness. The

Above: aubergines

Contents

Introduction

Mediterranean food is famously popular all over the world. The Mediterranean diet — rich in grains, vegetables, pulses, fruit and nuts, with little meat, plenty of fish, and olive oil as the main fat — has long been adopted as a model of healthy eating.

But its real appeal is the sensual quality of the cooking, which is full of rich flavours, aromas and colours, as well as its simplicity. It is the kind of food I love. I am sure you will want to adopt it for your everyday cooking, as well as for entertaining.

I have been travelling around the Mediterranean researching the cooking for decades now. I was born in Egypt and, as they say, if you belong to any part of the Mediterranean you are never a stranger along its shores. I feel at home with the architecture and the street life, the way people live, the way they shop and cook and eat. There is great regional diversity between the 16 or so countries around the Mediterranean, yet there are also many similarities. I found the same ingredients and many similar dishes from one end of the sea to the other. It has to do with the shared climate and produce, the age-old trading between the port cities, and an incestuous history, with the same empires and influences — Roman, Greek, Arab, Ottoman, Spanish — spreading across the region.

The recipes I picked for this book are some of the favourites I enjoyed on my travels and which I like to make at home. Dishes such as these, which have a history and are part of an old culture and tradition, have a special charm. You will love them too.

Ingredients and Equipment

INGREDIENTS

All ingredients used in Mediterranean cooking are generally available in the UK. Below is some useful information on the ingredients featured in this book.

Aubergines

The aubergine is the favourite vegetable of the Mediterranean. Choose firm, medium-sized ones with shiny, unblemished skin. If you are not going to fry them, you do not need to salt them to remove their bitter juices. The aubergines produced these days are only pleasantly bitter. Salting them does, however, mean that they absorb a little less oil, which is an advantage as they normally soak up so much. Grilling and roasting aubergines is a good way of avoiding that.

Bread

In the Mediterranean bread is present at every meal. It is used to pick up morsels of food, to dip into a creamy salad and to soak up sauces. It goes at the bottom of a juicy salad and in a bowl of soup; it is pounded into a sauce with olive oil; and crumbs are sprinkled over a gratin. The simplest appetizer in the western Mediterranean is a slice of bread smeared with olive oil and rubbed with garlic or tomatoes, or spread with an olive and anchovy paste.

The variety of breads that you find in the area, from the very thin, floppy breads baked on a griddle in the eastern Mediterranean to the great, round loaves of southern Italy, is extraordinary. The ever-increasing range available here is already substantial. Apart from the flat, pouched pitta, Italian ciabatta and focaccia, Spanish *pan gallego* and French baguette and country breads you can find in supermarkets, ethnic shops (mainly Turkish, Lebanese and Cypriot) and specialist bakeries now sell a wide variety of Mediterranean breads. There are different kinds of Lebanese flat breads, some exquisitely thin and light, some sprinkled with wild thyme, sesame seeds and sumac or flavoured with onions or garlic and herbs; Turkish sesame rings and huge, thick, soft, flat breads like focaccia; Greek olive breads and sesame loaves; Spanish *pan de borona* made with maize flour; Italian herb and olive oil and walnut and raisin breads.

Bulgur

Bulgur, a staple of Turkey and the Arab world, is wheat that has been boiled and dried, then ground to various degrees of fineness. The

Above: aubergines

Above: a selection of Mediterranean breads

Above: couscous (left), bulgur (right) and filo pastry underneath.

one available in supermarkets is medium-ground. It is used in salads and as a pilaf and is very easy to prepare, as it only needs to soak up water or stock and requires little or no cooking.

Capers

Capers are the pickled buds of a bush that grows wild in the Mediterranean. The best capers are preserved in salt rather than in brine or vinegar. Sometimes they are pickled on the branch, complete with thorns and leaves. They are good in salads and as a garnish for fish.

Cheeses

Mediterranean cheeses are made mostly from sheep's or goat's milk. They can be eaten for breakfast with olives, or as an appetizer – grilled, fried or simply cut into pieces. Feta and halloumi are the cheeses of the Middle East; pecorino, mozzarella and ricotta are used in southern Italy. The South of France produces a large selection of cheese for eating and uses Gruyère and Parmesan in cooking. Spanish cheeses include manchego, a firm sheep's milk cheese; the square, semi-soft mahon, made from cow's milk; and majorero, made from goat's milk.

The flavour of freshly grated Parmesan is far superior to that of the packaged, ready-grated type, so buy a piece and grate it as you need it – make sure you always buy Parmigiano Reggiano. It keeps in the refrigerator if you wrap it up well. Aged pecorino can be grated like Parmesan but it is very much sharper and is best used only in dishes featuring strong flavours.

Couscous

Couscous, a North African staple, is hard wheat that has been ground to various degrees of fineness, then moistened and coated with fine flour. It is traditionally cooked by lengthy steaming. The mass-produced varieties available in the UK are pre-cooked. They really only need to have water added (the same volume as its own) and to be heated through, but you can then make it light and fluffy by rubbing it between your hands.

Dried fruit

Sun-dried prunes, apricots, figs, raisins and currants are used in savoury dishes with meat and chicken as well as in sweet ones.

Filo pastry

A speciality of the eastern Mediterranean, this paper-thin pastry is now common all over the world. You can buy it fresh or frozen in supermarkets and some delicatessens. The sheets come in different sizes and different degrees of thinness.

Packs should not remain in the freezer for longer than three months, otherwise ice crystals form and, when these melt, the sheets stick together and tear when you try to separate them. Frozen filo must be allowed to defrost slowly for 2–3 hours. Open the packet just before you need it and then use the sheets as

Clockwise from bottom left: halloumi, Gruyère, Parmesan, mozzarella and feta

Clockwise from left: pickled/preserved lemons, green olives and kalamata olives

of a creamy soup, a stew or a tomato sauce and makes a rich dressing for pasta. For sauces that use plenty of oil, like mayonnaise, I mix a light vegetable oil such as sunflower with olive oil.

For deep-frying, use oils labelled refined olive oil or simply olive oil. These are produced from second or subsequent pressings, which have then been processed and refined and are usually quite bland. You can re-use olive oil after frying, but purify it by frying a lettuce leaf in it, then filter it to remove any bits before storing it in an airtight jar. Store olive oil in a cool place away from the light.

Olives

Olives are a symbol of the Mediterranean, and the limit of the olive tree defines the Mediterranean zone. They all ripen from green and yellow, through red and violet, to purple and black. Cured and preserved black and green olives are served for breakfast, as appetizers, and to accompany bread and cheese. They are also used in many different dishes. The main thing when buying olives is to pick a good-tasting variety. For this, you must sample them. Every Mediterranean country produces some very good ones. The fleshy Greek kalamata, the Spanish manzanilla and the large green Cerignola of Puglia, in Italy, are famous, as are the sweet, black, wrinkled olives of Provence and the tiny ones of Nice. Lately some very tasty Moroccan olives have come on the market.

Onions

The Mediterranean has many varieties of onion, including the fresh, white-bulbed ones, the smaller, more powerful ones, large Spanish and mild red Italian ones, shallots and spring onions. Many Mediterranean sauces and stews start with a base of chopped sautéed onions. They can also be braised, roasted, grilled or stuffed.

Orange-blossom water

The distilled essence of orange blossom adds a delicate perfume to many Mediterranean dishes and especially to the desserts of the eastern countries. In Morocco it is sometimes sprinkled over salads and also into stews. Use only a little, as it can be overpowering.

Pasta

Pasta is the everyday food of Italy, where there are reputedly 200 different kinds and shapes. Each type is said to make a difference to the taste as well as to the texture and appearance of the dish, because of the amount of sauce it is capable of collecting. It is best to buy dried pasta made with durum wheat, which preserves the wheatgerm, because this is the tastiest as well as the healthiest type. Its size trebles with cooking, it cooks evenly and does not get sticky.

Every country of the eastern Mediterranean also has some kind of pasta, in particular *rishta* (noodles), *lissan al assfour* (birds' tongues), which are added to meat stews, and *itriya* and *shaghria* (spaghetti and vermicelli), which are cooked with rice or served with a yoghurt topping, or cooked in milk with sugar for a pudding. Turkish *manti*, a stuffed pasta, is like the Chinese wonton and is Mongolian in origin.

Peppers

Like aubergines, peppers are one of the great vegetables of the Mediterranean. Red and yellow peppers are more mature than green ones, and the red ones are the sweetest. When they are roasted they acquire a lovely texture and delicious flavour. Choose firm, fleshy peppers.

Pickled or preserved lemons

You can now find lemons preserved in brine in some supermarkets. They give a distinctive flavour to Moroccan and North African *tagines* (stews) and salads. One variety of small, thin-skinned preserved lemon called *beldi* is particularly good. Normally the peel alone is used but some people like to throw in the pulp as well, especially with the very small ones.

Pulses

Pulses such as chickpeas, broad beans, lentils, haricot beans, black-eyed beans, borlotti and cannellini beans, and yellow and green split

SOUPS and STARTERS

Chilled almond soup with garlic and grapes

This is another popular Andalusian soup, which is called *ajo blanco* (white garlic). There is meant to be a lot of garlic, and it is raw, but you can reduce the quantity if you prefer. Crush it in a garlic press or pound it to a paste with a little salt in a mortar. Choose good white bread from a country-style loaf and a mild-tasting extra-virgin olive oil. I always used to peel the grapes but recently I have stopped doing that and found the result just as good. You can make the soup several hours in advance.

serves 4
preparation time: 25 minutes

100 g (4 oz) day-old white bread, cut into slices, crusts removed

250 g (9 oz) blanched almonds

3 garlic cloves, crushed

500 ml (17 fl oz) iced water

120 ml (4 fl oz) extra-virgin olive oil, plus a little extra to serve

3 tablespoons sherry vinegar or white wine vinegar, or to taste

300 g (11 oz) white seedless grapes, or more, washed

salt

1 Put the bread in a small bowl, pour over just enough water to cover and leave to soak for a few minutes.

2 Grind the almonds very finely in a food processor. Squeeze the bread dry and add to the almonds with the garlic and a few tablespoons of the iced water. Process to a smooth paste.

3 With the food processor still running, add the olive oil in a slow stream. Then add the remaining cold water until the soup has a creamy consistency.

4 Pour into a serving bowl, season with salt and vinegar and stir in the grapes. Cover with cling film and chill for at least an hour. Serve drizzled with a little oil.

Spiced lentil soup

Lentil soup is an Egyptian favourite and part of my childhood memories. This homely version is simple and heart-warming.

serves 4
preparation time: 10 minutes
cooking time: 35–50 minutes

1 onion, chopped

1¹/₂ tablespoons olive oil

2 garlic cloves, crushed

³/₄ teaspoon ground cumin

³/₄ teaspoon ground coriander

150 g (5 oz) split red lentils

1.25 litres (2¹/₄ pints) chicken
   stock (you may use 1¹/₂–2
   stock cubes)

juice of ¹/₂ lemon

salt and pepper

1 Fry the onion in the oil in a large saucepan until soft, stirring occasionally.

2 Stir in the garlic, cumin and coriander. When the aroma rises (in moments only), add the lentils and stock.

3 Bring to the boil and skim off any scum that appears on the surface. Reduce the heat and simmer for 30–45 minutes, until the lentils have disintegrated. Add salt if necessary (taking into account the saltiness of the stock cubes) and some pepper.

4 Thin with a little water if necessary. Stir in the lemon juice before serving.

Aubergine caviar

Often described as 'poor man's caviar', this is the commonest way of eating aubergines all around the Mediterranean. Use firm, medium-sized aubergines with a shiny black skin. The texture is better if you chop the flesh by hand rather than blending it in a food processor. If you want to prepare a large quantity for a party, instead of grilling the aubergines you can roast them in the hottest possible oven (lay them on a sheet of foil) for about 30 minutes, turning them on their side at least once.

serves 4
preparation time: 15 minutes
cooking time: about 15 minutes

2 aubergines, weighing
   approximately 675 g
   (1¹/₂ lb) in total
4 tablespoons extra-virgin
   olive oil
juice of ¹/₂ lemon, or more
   to taste
salt
chopped fresh parsley or
   black olives, to garnish
   (optional)

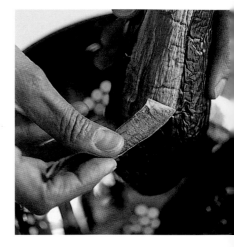

1 Prick the aubergines in a few places with a sharp knife to prevent them bursting. Place them under a hot grill and cook, turning occasionally, until they feel very soft and the skin is wrinkled.

2 Peel the aubergines, letting the flesh fall into a fine colander or a sieve. Chop the flesh with a sharp knife and mash to a purée with a fork or a wooden spoon, so that the juices escape through the holes of the colander or sieve.

3 Transfer the purée to a bowl and beat in the oil, lemon juice and some salt to taste. Garnish with chopped parsley or black olives before serving, if liked.

Carrot and potato appetizer

This homely Tunisian salad is easy to make and very tasty. Use old carrots and mealy potatoes. Serve it cold, with bread or toast for dipping.

serves 4

preparation time: 15 minutes

675 g (1½ lb) carrots, peeled

500 g (1 lb 2 oz) potatoes, peeled

2 garlic cloves, chopped

3–4 teaspoons ground cumin

5 tablespoons extra-virgin olive oil

2 tablespoons wine vinegar

a large pinch of chilli powder or cayenne pepper

salt

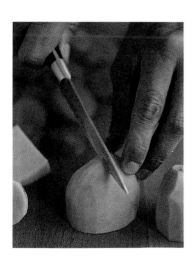

1 Slice the carrots and cut each potato into 2–4 pieces. Put them in a pan with some salt, the garlic and enough water to cover.

2 Bring to the boil, then reduce the heat and simmer until soft. Drain well and mash with a potato masher or a fork.

3 Put the carrot and potato purée in a serving bowl and stir in the remaining ingredients, adding more salt if necessary.

Bulgur and tomato salad

Kisir is a luscious and filling Turkish country salad. A touch of chilli gives it a thrilling zing. The bulgur does not need cooking, only soaking in water until it is tender.

serves 6–8
preparation time: 30 minutes,
plus 20 minutes' standing

250 g (9 oz) bulgur (cracked wheat)

2 tablespoons tomato purée

5 tablespoons extra-virgin olive oil

juice of 1 lemon

1/3 teaspoon dried chilli flakes or a pinch of chilli powder, or to taste

1 fresh red or green chilli, very finely chopped

5 tablespoons chopped fresh flat-leaf parsley

3 sprigs of fresh mint, chopped

6 spring onions, finely chopped

2 large tomatoes, finely diced

salt

1 Put the bulgur in a bowl, pour plenty of boiling water over it and leave to stand for 20 minutes, or until the grain is just tender.

2 Drain the bulgur through a fine sieve or colander and squeeze the excess water out.

3 Add the tomato purée, oil, lemon juice, chilli flakes or powder and some salt and mix thoroughly. You can do this in advance.

4 Just before serving, mix in all
the remaining ingredients.

Greek country salad

This salad can be prepared in advance but it should be dressed only at the last minute. I like it kept simple, but possible additions are chopped fennel, wild marjoram, sprigs of mint, capers and sliced gherkins. Serve with good country bread.

serves 6
preparation time: 25 minutes

1 cos lettuce

2 large, ripe but firm tomatoes

1 cucumber

1 green pepper

1 large, mild red or white
   onion or 9 spring onions

250 g (9 oz) feta cheese,
   cut into small squares or
   broken into coarse pieces

12 or more black kalamata
   olives

For the dressing:

a good bunch of fresh flat-
   leaf parsley, coarsely
   chopped

6 tablespoons extra-virgin
   olive oil

juice of 1 lemon

salt and pepper

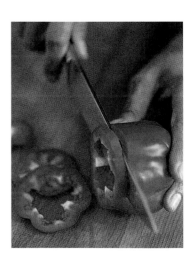

1 Shred the lettuce into wide ribbons with a sharp knife. Cut the tomatoes into wedges. Peel the cucumber, cut it lengthways in half, then slice it thickly.

2 Remove the seeds from the green pepper and cut it into thin rings. If using 1 large onion, slice it thinly and separate the rings; if using spring onions, just slice them thinly.

3 Put the prepared vegetables into a large bowl with the feta cheese and olives.

4 Just before serving, mix all the ingredients for the dressing together. Pour the dressing over the salad and toss well.

3 Roast the peppers for another 15 minutes, or until the skins are browned and they feel soft, turning them once. Drop them into a plastic freezer bag and twist to close it; this loosens the skins further. When they are cool enough to handle, peel the peppers and remove the seeds, then cut each pepper into 8 ribbons from the stem end to the bottom.

5 Arrange the elements of the salad – onions, peppers, tomatoes, flaked tuna and eggs – on individual plates in a decorative way. A garnish of capers, olives and anchovies is optional. Mix the oil, lemon juice, salt, pepper and caraway seeds together and drizzle over the salad.

4 Take the onions out when they feel soft when you press them. They will take 15–30 minutes longer than the peppers. Leave until cool enough to handle, then peel them and cut into wedges.

Roasted peppers and aubergines with yoghurt

Peppers and aubergines are the most popular vegetables around the Mediterranean and this is my favourite way of cooking them. I serve them hot as a side dish or cold as an appetizer. Yoghurt is a traditional Turkish accompaniment.

serves 4

preparation time: about 20 minutes

cooking time: about 15 minutes

2 medium-sized aubergines, weighing approximately 675 g (1½ lb) in total

2 fleshy red peppers

3 tablespoons extra-virgin olive oil

300 ml (10 fl oz) natural yoghurt or thick, Greek-style yoghurt

1 garlic clove, crushed (optional)

salt

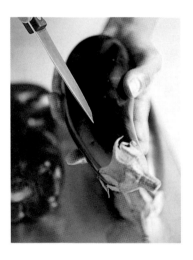
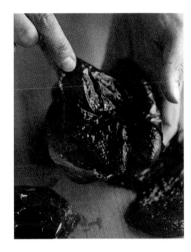

1 Prick the aubergines in a few places with a sharp knife to prevent them exploding. Place the aubergines and peppers on a piece of foil on a baking sheet and place under a hot grill (or put the vegetables directly on a barbecue grill over glowing embers).

2 Cook the peppers for about 10 minutes, turning them occasionally, until they soften and the skin is blackened and blistered. Put them in a plastic freezer bag (thinner plastic can melt with the heat), twist it closed and leave for 15–20 minutes (this helps to loosen the skins further; another way is to put them in a pan with a tight-fitting lid). When the peppers are cool enough to handle, peel them and remove the stems and seeds.

4 Cut the peppers and aubergines into wide strips, sprinkle lightly with salt and the olive oil and mix gently. If serving hot, heat through in the oven first. Accompany with the yoghurt, mixed, if you like, with the garlic.

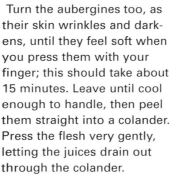

3 Turn the aubergines too, as their skin wrinkles and darkens, until they feel soft when you press them with your finger; this should take about 15 minutes. Leave until cool enough to handle, then peel them straight into a colander. Press the flesh very gently, letting the juices drain out through the colander.

ROASTED PEPPERS AND AUBERGINES WITH YOGHURT | 49

FISH and SHELLFISH

Red mullet in a saffron and ginger tomato sauce

Fish cooked in tomato sauce is ubiquitous in every Mediterranean country. This exquisitely flavoured sauce may also be used with other kinds of fish – small whole ones or fillets such as haddock, cod or salmon. If you find small red mullet, it is lovely to use them whole.

I extract the juice from fresh ginger by peeling it, cutting it into small pieces and crushing them in a garlic press, but you can just grate the ginger if you prefer.

serves 2
preparation time: 25 minutes
cooking time: about 20 minutes

3 garlic cloves, chopped

1 fresh chilli, finely chopped

2–3 tablespoons extra-virgin olive oil

500 g (1 lb 2 oz) ripe tomatoes, skinned and chopped

1½ teaspoons sugar

¼ teaspoon crushed saffron strands (see page 20) or saffron powder

4 cm (1½ in) piece of fresh root ginger, the juice squeezed out in a garlic press

2 medium-sized red mullet, cleaned and filleted

salt and pepper

1 In a frying pan, heat the garlic and chilli in the olive oil for moments only, stirring, until the aroma rises.

2 Add the tomatoes, sugar, saffron, ginger juice and some salt and pepper and simmer for 10 minutes.

3 Put the red mullet fillets in the tomato sauce and simmer for up to 6 minutes, turning the fish over once, until the flesh begins to flake when you cut into it with a sharp knife.

Cod with salsa verde

Salsa verde, a strongly flavoured Italian green sauce, makes a good accompaniment to cod. It also goes well with other white fish, such as haddock, halibut and monkfish, and with salmon and salmon trout. It is served at room temperature and keeps for days in the refrigerator. The fish can be grilled or poached in white wine but the simplest way to cook it is in a frying pan.

serves 4
preparation time: 15 minutes
cooking time: 4–10 minutes

3 tablespoons olive oil

4 x 150 g (5 oz) pieces of cod fillet, skinned

salt

For the salsa verde:

a very large bunch of fresh flat-leaf parsley, weighing about 50 g (2 oz), stalks removed

75 g (3 oz) pine nuts

5 small cocktail gherkins

8 green olives, pitted

2–3 garlic cloves, crushed

3 tablespoons wine vinegar or the juice of 1/2 lemon

about 120 ml (4 fl oz) mild extra-virgin olive oil

salt and pepper

1 Prepare the salsa verde first. Blend all the ingredients except the oil in a food processor. Then add the extra-virgin olive oil gradually – enough to give a creamy paste. Taste and adjust the seasoning if necessary.

2 Heat the olive oil in a large, preferably non-stick, frying pan that will hold the cod in one layer. Put in the fish and sprinkle with salt.

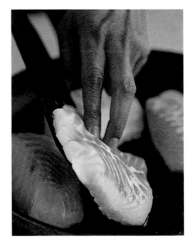

3 Cook over a low heat for 4–10 minutes (depending on the thickness of the fish), turning the fish over once and sprinkling it with salt. It is ready when the flesh is opaque and just begins to flake if you cut into it with a sharp knife. Serve accompanied by the sauce.

Spicy prawns

This Moroccan way with prawns is quick to prepare and tastes wonderful. Use raw king prawns (they are grey and turn pink when cooked). Some supermarkets sell them ready peeled. You can also buy them frozen with their heads off from some fishmongers, in which case you may need double the weight.

serves 4
preparation time: 20 minutes
cooking time: about 3 minutes

600 g (1 lb 5 oz) raw king prawns, shell on, or 300 g (11 oz) peeled ones

4 tablespoons extra-virgin olive oil

4 garlic cloves, crushed

2 teaspoons paprika

1½ teaspoons ground cumin

¾ teaspoon ground ginger

a good pinch of cayenne pepper or chilli powder

5 tablespoons chopped fresh coriander or parsley

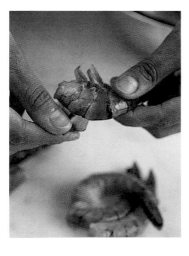

1 To peel the prawns, twist off their heads and pull off the 'legs'. Then break open the shell along the belly and peel it off (leave the tail on, if liked, for more attractive presentation). If you see a dark thread along the back, make a fine slit with a sharp knife and pull it out.

2 In a large frying pan, heat the oil with the garlic and spices, stirring, for seconds only, until the aroma rises.

3 Throw in the peeled prawns and fry quickly over a medium heat, stirring and turning them over, for about 1 minute, until they turn pink. Stir in the coriander or parsley towards the end.

Provençal prawns

Cognac and white wine give this sauce an exquisite flavour. It is very good served with rice. Use raw king prawns, either with the shells still on or ready peeled. If you buy frozen prawns with their heads off, you may need double the weight.

serves 4
preparation time: 30 minutes
cooking time: 30 minutes

600 g (1 lb 5 oz) raw king prawns, shell on, or 300 g (11 oz) peeled ones

1 onion, chopped

2 tablespoons extra-virgin olive oil

2 garlic cloves, finely chopped

500 g (1 lb 2 oz) tomatoes, skinned and chopped

1 teaspoon sugar

1 fresh red chilli, finely chopped

3 tablespoons cognac

150 ml (5 fl oz) dry white wine

2 sprigs of fresh thyme

1 bay leaf

3 tablespoons chopped fresh flat-leaf parsley

salt

1 To peel the prawns, twist off their heads and pull off the 'legs'. Then break open the shell along the belly and peel it off (leave the tail on, if liked, for more attractive presentation). If you see a dark thread along the back, make a fine slit with a sharp knife and pull it out.

2 Fry the onion in the olive oil in a large frying pan, stirring occasionally, until it begins to colour.

3 Add the garlic and, when the aroma rises, add all the remaining ingredients except the prawns and parsley. Simmer, uncovered, for about 20 minutes, until the sauce is reduced and aromatic.

4 Add the prawns and cook over a medium heat for 1–2 minutes, turning them over, until they turn pink. Serve hot, garnished with the parsley.

POULTRY and MEAT

Chicken with rosemary

This Italian way of cooking chicken is so simple that you could easily adopt it for every day. Serve with boiled or mashed potatoes.

serves 4
preparation time: 10 minutes
cooking time: about 40 minutes

40g (1¹/₂ oz) butter

1 tablespoon extra-virgin olive oil

2–3 garlic cloves, cut in half

2 sprigs of fresh rosemary

1 chicken, weighing about 1.5 kg (3 lb), cut into quarters

175 ml (6 fl oz) dry white wine

salt and pepper

1 Heat the butter and oil in a large shallow frying pan with the garlic and rosemary.

2 When the mixture sizzles, put in the chicken and cook over a medium heat, turning the pieces, until they are coloured all over.

3 Sprinkle the chicken with salt and pepper, add the wine, then cover and simmer for 30 minutes, or until the chicken is very tender.

Poussins in a honey sauce with couscous stuffing

Like many festive dishes in Morocco, this is savoury and sweet. Some of the couscous stuffing goes inside the birds, the rest is to serve on the side. You could make it easier for yourself by serving it all on the side. A small poussin is not too much for one person but a large one should be cut in half to serve two.

Couscous is made from durum semolina. The traditional way of cooking it is by lengthy steaming. However, the commercial variety available in the UK has been pre-cooked and only needs water added and heating through.

serves 4

preparation time: 25 minutes, plus 15 minutes' standing time for the couscous

cooking time: 45–60 minutes

4 small poussins

40 g (1¹/₂ oz) butter or 3 tablespoons sunflower oil

1¹/₂ large onions, finely chopped or grated

2 garlic cloves, crushed

2 teaspoons ground cinnamon

¹/₄ teaspoon ground ginger

¹/₂ teaspoon crushed saffron strands or saffron powder (see page 20)

2 tablespoons honey

salt and plenty of pepper

For the couscous stuffing:

350 g (12 oz) couscous

¹/₂–³/₄ teaspoon salt

2–3 teaspoons caster sugar

2¹/₂ tablespoons sunflower oil

1 teaspoon ground cinnamon

1¹/₂ tablespoons orange-blossom water

50 g (2 oz) blanched almonds

50 g (2 oz) pistachio nuts

2 tablespoons raisins, soaked in warm water for 10 minutes and then drained

25 g (1 oz) butter

1 Prepare the stuffing first. Measure the volume of couscous in a measuring jug, then pour it into a bowl. Measure the same volume of warm water in the jug and mix in the salt. Add to the couscous and stir well so that the water is evenly absorbed. Leave to stand for about 15 minutes.

Chicken with pickled lemons and olives

I love the taste of lemons pickled (or preserved) in salt. They lose their sharpness and acquire a special flavour. At every vegetable market in North Africa, and now also in the south of France, there are stalls laden with huge piles of soft lemons, oozing with juice, next to several varieties of olives. The two are often used together. You can now find pickled lemons and Moroccan olives in supermarkets. In this recipe the lemon is added towards the end of cooking but some cooks like to use a little chopped lemon to flavour the sauce during the cooking.

serves 4
preparation time: 20 minutes
cooking time: about 45 minutes

1 large chicken, cut into quarters

3 tablespoons vegetable oil or extra-virgin olive oil

1 large onion, grated or very finely chopped

2–3 garlic cloves, crushed

1/4 teaspoon crushed saffron strands (see page 20) or saffron powder

1/2 – 3/4 teaspoon ground ginger

1 1/2 teaspoons ground cinnamon

1 1/2 large or 3 small pickled lemons, rinsed and cut into quarters or thin strips

12–16 green or violet olives, soaked in 2 changes of water for 30 minutes and then drained

salt and pepper

1 Put the chicken pieces in a large, wide saucepan with all the ingredients except the preserved lemons and the olives. Half cover with water and bring just to the boil.

2 Reduce the heat, then cover the pan and simmer for about 45 minutes, until the chicken is so tender that the flesh can be pulled off the bone easily and the liquid is reduced to a thick sauce. Turn the chicken pieces over a few times during cooking and add a little more water if necessary.

3 Stir the lemon peel and olives into the sauce for the last 15 minutes of cooking. Some people like to add the lemon right at the very end.

Chicken with tomatoes and honey

This Moroccan *tagine* is one of my favourites. The chicken cooks in the juice from the tomatoes, which reduces to a sumptuous, thick, honeyed — almost caramelized — sauce. And it looks beautiful, too. Don't be worried about the large quantity of tomatoes; they will reduce right down.

One of the peculiarities of the Moroccan style of cooking — and of Fez in particular — is that they put all the ingredients in the pot at the same time, rather than frying the basic flavourings in the oil first.

serves 4
preparation time: 30 minutes
cooking time: about 1 1/4 hours

1 large chicken, cut into quarters

3 tablespoons sunflower oil or vegetable oil

1 large onion, grated or finely chopped

1 kg (2 1/4 lb) tomatoes, skinned and chopped

1/2 teaspoon ground ginger

1 teaspoon ground cinnamon

1/2 teaspoon crushed saffron strands (see page 20) or saffron powder

2 tablespoons clear (liquid) honey, or to taste (Moroccans use up to 4 tablespoons)

50 g (2 oz) blanched almonds, coarsely chopped

1 tablespoon sesame seeds

salt and pepper

1 Put all the ingredients except the honey, almonds, sesame seeds and 1 tablespoon of the oil in a large pan. Cover and cook over a low heat, turning the chicken pieces over occasionally, for about 1 hour, until the flesh is so tender that it can be pulled off the bone easily.

2 Remove the chicken pieces from the pan and keep warm. Cook the sauce over a medium heat until it has reduced to a thick, sizzling cream. Stir as it begins to caramelize and be careful that it does not stick or burn. Stir in the honey. Return the chicken pieces to the sauce and heat through.

3 Heat the chopped almonds in the remaining oil in a frying pan for moments only, then add the sesame seeds and stir them over a low heat for a few moments, until lightly coloured. Serve the chicken hot, covered with the sauce and sprinkled with the almonds and sesame seeds.

Sautéed pork medallions with Marsala

This Sicilian dish could not be easier. Use a sweet Marsala wine rather than a dry one. Serve with mashed or boiled potatoes.

serves 4
preparation time: 5 minutes
cooking time: about 10 minutes

2 pork fillets, weighing
   approximately 1 kg (2¼ lb)
   in total
4 tablespoons sunflower oil
150 ml (5 fl oz) Marsala
salt and pepper

1 Cut the pork fillets into medallion slices about 1 cm (½ in) thick.

2 Heat the sunflower oil in a large frying pan, add the pieces of meat and sauté quickly over a high heat until browned on both sides.

3 Sprinkle with salt and pepper and pour in the Marsala. Cook for a few minutes, until the meat is cooked through and the liquid has reduced a little. Serve immediately.

SAUTEED PORK MEDALLIONS WITH MARSALA | 89

Greek stifatho

This heart-warming winter stew takes a long time to cook but does not need to be watched. It is peeling a large number of baby onions that is time-consuming. You will need a very large pan or casserole to cook the stew in. Serve with crusty bread, rice or potatoes.

serves 6–8
preparation time: 25 minutes
cooking time: about 2 hours

1 kg (2¼ lb) small pickling onions

1 kg (2¼ lb) stewing beef (or brisket) or pork, cut into 4 cm (1½ in) cubes

1 bottle of red wine

6 peppercorns

5 cloves

½–1 teaspoon ground allspice

4 tablespoons red or white wine vinegar

4 tablespoons extra-virgin olive oil

salt

1 Poach the pickling onions in a large pan of boiling water for 2–3 minutes to loosen their skins and make peeling easier. Then drain and peel them.

2 Put all the ingredients in a large pan or casserole and barely cover with water. Bring to the boil and skim off any scum that gathers on the surface.

3 Cover the pan and simmer over a very low heat for about 2 hours, or until the meat is very tender, adding more water if necessary to keep the meat just covered. Taste and adjust the seasoning, then serve.

2 Meanwhile, make the meatballs. Mix together the
minced meat, onion, parsley,
spices and some salt and
pepper and gently knead to a
soft paste with your hands.

3 Rub your hands with a little
oil so that the meat does not
stick, then roll the mixture
into marble-sized balls and
place them side by side on
a plate.

4 Heat a thin layer of vegetable
oil in a large frying pan and
fry the meatballs briefly in it
in batches, shaking the pan
and turning the meatballs to
brown them all over. They
should still be pink inside.
Lift out with a slotted spoon
and leave to drain on kitchen
paper.

5 Add the parsley and coriander to the sauce, put in the meatballs and simmer for about 5 minutes, until they are cooked through.

6 Break the eggs over the sauce and cook until the whites have set. Serve immediately.

PASTA, GRAINS and VEGETABLES

Bulgur pilaf

Bulgur (cracked wheat) makes satisfying comfort food. It is quick and easy to prepare and can be served as a side dish. It is something I am sure you will want to adopt. Use either the coarse-ground bulgur, found in Middle Eastern shops, or the medium-ground one that is now commonly available in supermarkets. About one and a half times the volume of water or stock is needed. You can measure it by the cup if you want to make only a small quantity. Adding the optional currants or raisins and pine nuts gives a richer version, but the simple, plain one is also delicious.

serves 6–8
preparation time: 10 minutes,
  plus 10 minutes' standing time
cooking time: 10–15 minutes

1 litre (1³/₄ pints) water or chicken stock (you may use 2 stock cubes)

500 g (1 lb 2 oz) coarse- or medium-ground bulgur

65 g (2¹/₂ oz) butter, cut into small pieces, or 5 tablespoons vegetable oil

50 g (2 oz) currants or raisins, soaked in water and drained (optional)

100 g (4 oz) pine nuts, toasted (optional)

salt and pepper

1 Bring the water or stock to the boil in a large pan and add the bulgur.

2 Add some salt and pepper, stir well and cook, covered, over a low heat for 10–15 minutes, until the grain is almost tender and all the liquid has been absorbed, adding a little more water if it becomes too dry.

3 Stir in the butter or oil, then remove the pan from the heat and leave to stand, covered, for about 10 minutes to allow the wheat to swell and become tender before serving. If using the currants or raisins and pine nuts, fold them in gently at the same time as the butter or oil.

Stuffed mushrooms

This is a Provençal and Ligurian way of preparing mushrooms. It makes an ideal first course or side dish. The French put in cognac, Italians often use rum.

serves 3–6
preparation time: 10 minutes
cooking time: 25 minutes

6 large, flat Portabello mushrooms

extra-virgin olive oil

2 good slices of white bread,
crusts removed

5 tablespoons finely chopped
fresh parsley

2–3 garlic cloves, crushed

3 tablespoons cognac

salt and pepper

1 Pre-heat the oven to 200°C/400°F/Gas Mark 6. Wipe the mushrooms with a damp cloth, if necessary. Cut off the stalks and set aside.

2 Heat a thin layer of olive oil in a large frying pan and sauté the mushrooms briefly over a medium heat for about 5 minutes, sprinkling lightly with salt and pepper and turning them over once. Arrange them, stem side up, in a flat, heatproof dish.

3 To make the stuffing, chop the mushroom stalks and crumble the bread finely. You can do this in a food processor, if you like, with the parsley.

4 Place the mushroom stalks, bread and parsley in a bowl and add as much garlic as you like, plus a little salt and pepper. Moisten with the cognac and 3–4 tablespoons of olive oil and mix well.

5 Press a little stuffing over each mushroom and bake for about 20 minutes, or until the mushrooms are tender.